OCRACOKE PORTRAIT

"It furthers one to cross the great water."

OCRACOKE PORTRAIT

Photographs and Interviews By
Ann Sebrell Ehringhaus

John F. Blair, Publisher
Winston-Salem, North Carolina

Part of the author's proceeds from the sale of this book
will be donated to the Ocracoke School photography
program and the Ocracoke Preservation Society.

Cover photograph, "Heading In," hand-tinted by the author.
Typesetting by Typography Studio, Inc., Winston-Salem, North Carolina.
Manufactured by BookCrafters.

Quotations have been edited only for clarity. They do not
necessarily appear beside the person who made them.
Speakers are identified in the last section of the book.

Library of Congress Cataloging in Publication Data

Ehringhaus, Ann Sebrell, 1949-
    Ocracoke portrait/photographs and interviews by
Ann Sebrell Ehringhaus.
        p.   cm.
    ISBN 0-89587-060-6
    ISBN 0-89587-061-4 (pbk.)
      1. Ocracoke Island (N.C.)—Description and travel—Views.
    2. Ocracoke Island (N.C.)—Social life and customs—Pictorial works.
    I. Title.
F262.H9E37 1988   88‑10483
975.6'197—dc19   CIP

*Dedicated to the wonder
of the island and to the
islanders and all others
who have felt a sense of
belonging here.*

Contents

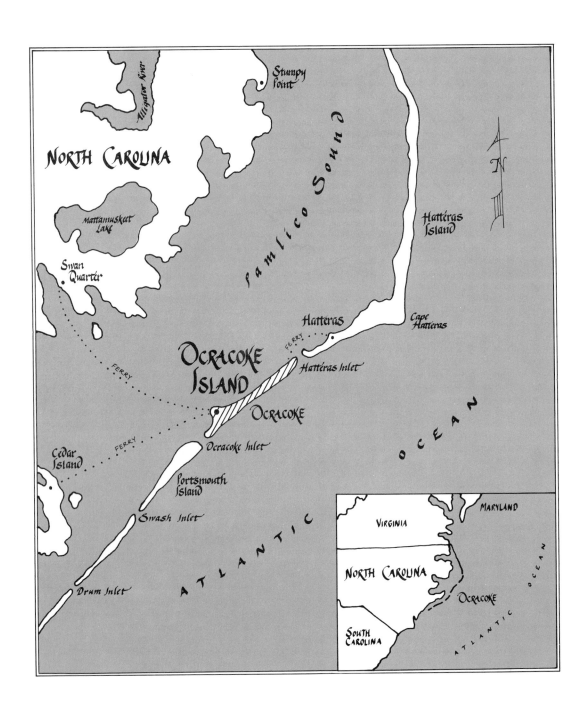

Preface

I first saw Ocracoke in 1971 with the eyes of a twenty-two-year-old school-teacher. I had never been on a true island—land reached only by ferry—and had little real knowledge of people. I was educated in the ways of school but not in the ways of life. I had never lived in a place dominated by the weather. The island's sturdy fragility, its earthy magic and strong feelings of past times and people enchanted me then, as they do today. Through the years, Ocracoke has shown me both what it means to be part of a community and how important it is to be self-sufficient. It has taught me the value of finding a balance within the environment as well as within myself.

My desire to make a visual portrait of the island emerged in 1979, after I had completed my formal study of photography. Working on the documentation process put me at the pulse of the island—not a bad place to be. These pictures tell a story of physical activity and emotional closeness. They give a feeling for the space on the island and for the importance of details. There is time for details here.

I decided to interview people and let their voices tell a story of Ocracoke. Some are islanders or current residents, and others merely crossed my path for an hour or a day. The first interview was conducted at the Ocracoke campground, where I lived under the sky and stars for a week to collect my thoughts for the completion of this book. Later, after a month of interviewing, I began to hear *every* spoken word or phrase as a quote. In the post office one day I remarked to a tourist on the humidity, and he replied, "I hate the humidity, but I love Ocracoke, been coming here since 1968." Commentary at the mailbox. Truly, I found it everywhere, with everyone I interviewed. I guess you live or even vacation twenty-three miles offshore for philosophical reasons. I had been thinking I would get anecdotes, while what I often got were reflections and personal realizations.

People at Ocracoke must continually *choose* to be here, for in many ways life is hard and lacks luxuries and diversions most people take for granted. There is a resilience about island people; they are survivors, but with a special sense of humor. They never miss a chance for a practical joke or a good story. People can be themselves at Ocracoke, with all the good and bad that implies. People feel connected with the natural world; it is part of them. They can feel rain coming, and they can sense the movements of fish and fowl. Since the lives of many Ocracokers depend upon challenging the treacherous waters nearby, they have a special sense of the interrelatedness of life and death.

The time to preserve and protect this island life is now. This fall an islander said to me, "I'm homesick for the island, and I'm here." We must not let the goodness slip away. My respect and love for this place and its people grow deeper with each passing season. I believe that the connection between people and their environment is important, and nowhere is this more evident than Ocracoke. I believe that preservation of natural resources and island history must be a conscious choice; it will not happen accidentally. The island will change, but its rich and unique past should shape its future.

This book is a visual testament to the natural beauty and closeness of life here. May the voices and pictures speak through the pages and touch you with what they understand of the mystery.

Acknowledgments

I wish to thank the many islanders who participated in the making of this book. We have traded fish and crabs for photographs for years. All photographs were made from 1979 to 1987 with a Mamiya C220 2 ¼-inch camera, Plus-X film, and a variety of filters. These photographs were made as part of *living* at Ocracoke. They were not considered a separate activity; they were neither posed nor pre-arranged. While walking, riding, or boating, there would suddenly be a moment when all the pieces fit together, when something would ring out. This moment became a photograph. I wish to thank the island of Ocracoke—a place where there are many moments that ring true.

Other thanks through the years go to:

Alice and Emmett Sebrell, my parents, who showed me a long time ago that beaches and boats were the two best places to be,

Diane Gooch, wherever she is, for telling me in 1971 of "some island off the coast" that needed two teachers,

Michael Ehringhaus, whose spirit of adventure matched mine, and who dared to move to the island with me,

Ocracoke School students from 1971 to 1973, who shared their island's way of life and sense of humor,

The New England School of Photography in Boston, Massachusetts, for giving me experiences, techniques, ideas, and feelings to consider throughout my life,

The Simpson House, behind the Ocracoke lighthouse, where this project began,

The Light Factory photographic community of Charlotte, North Carolina, whose friendship, interest, and support have been ongoing. Special thanks to Howard Spector and Mark Sloan, past directors of the Light Factory, and to Ken Bloom, current director,

Dave Crosby, Bill Burlingame, Doug MacLean, and Holly Rogers, long-time friends whose friendship doesn't seem to diminish no matter how far offshore I get,

Mike Hays, who helped me to establish a real home on Ocracoke and who has given much encouragement through the years,

The many strong, caring, and independent women who live on Ocracoke and whose lives and friendships remain an inspiration for me,

Willis Slane, Kathy Jordan, Debbie Wells, my sister Alice Sebrell, and Cynthia Mitchell, who were of particular help in the book's final stages and who have all talked and shared ideas and given direction and love,

The Appalachian Environmental Arts Center in Highlands, North Carolina—a program of the University of North Carolina—and Director Gil Leebrick, for providing time and space in a beautiful place where I could complete this book,

And Margaret, Carolyn, Debbie, and Steve at John F. Blair, Publisher, for their personal interest, assistance, and encouragement in this book project.

Introduction

Your journey to Ocracoke will be an adventure you never forget.

Part of the legendary barrier island chain known as North Carolina's Outer Banks, Ocracoke is a small island washed by the Atlantic Ocean and Pamlico Sound. Ocracoke measures approximately sixteen miles in length and varies from one-half to two miles in width, and is reached only by private plane or state-operated ferryboat. Ferryboats are an important part of recent island history. Today, boats leave the mainland ports of Cedar Island and Swan Quarter several times daily, carrying thirty to fifty cars for the two-and-a-half-hour crossing to the island. Boats also depart hourly from Hatteras Island for the forty-five-minute trip across Hatteras Inlet.

Ocracoke Village, with its year-round population of 657, is situated around Silver Lake harbor at the southern end of the island. Less than nine hundred acres of the island are privately owned, with the northernmost fifteen miles of the island owned and maintained by the National Park Service. A sense of history pervades the little island village, even as touches of the modern world appear alongside the old.

When Europeans arrived on Ocracoke in 1585, the island was inhabited by Indians and was known as "Wokokon," meaning "fort." Maps show that the island's name evolved into its current spelling much as the island itself evolved into its present shape. A map from 1585 shows Ocracoke only eight miles long, separated from Hatteras Island by the old Hatteras Inlet, which closed in the 1750s. Ocracoke and Hatteras remained attached until 1846, when the present Hatteras Inlet was cut by a hurricane.

The first official settlement of the island occurred in 1715, when the North Carolina General Assembly passed an act to settle seafaring pilots on Ocracoke to guide shipping vessels through the treacherous Ocracoke Inlet. This early settlement was known as "Pilot Town." Unofficial settlers around the island at that time were Blackbeard and a variety of other pirates. Pirates often posed as pilots and "lightened" ships of valuable cargo before leading them aground on shallow shoals in the inlet.

Edward Teach, the man better known as Blackbeard, met his infamous death just off Ocracoke. On the morning of November 22, 1718, British Lieutenant Robert Maynard entered Ocracoke Inlet and ran aground. Blackbeard and his pirates fired on Maynard and then boarded his ship, thinking most of the crew were dead. Maynard was hunting for Blackbeard, however, and he had hidden his crew below decks. A deadly battle ensued. Blackbeard absorbed repeated injuries before he died. Maynard chopped off Blackbeard's head as evidence of his victory, and legend tells that the pirate's body swam around the ship seven times before sinking. Many people wonder if Blackbeard's treasure is still buried somewhere around Ocracoke. The location of this deadly duel has become legend—"Teach's Hole" is definitely a notorious fishing spot!

Many islanders believe that World War II brought the first major changes in the way of life on Ocracoke. Until the late 1930s, Ocracokers were still living on sandy lanes without electricity. Wartime saw the construction of a large navy base and the paving of many lanes for access to ammunition dump sites. Many of these concrete roads are still in use today. The navy also dredged Silver Lake to allow deep-water vessels into the harbor, and by dumping the dredged sand created the only hill on the island. This wartime influx of fifteen hundred to two thousand people forever changed the quiet little village of Ocracoke, as many islanders took boarders into their homes, and many of the sailors married local girls and took them away from the island.

Islanders remember curfews when no one was allowed on the beach after dark. They remember seeing burning vessels offshore and fearing that spies were living among them. During the war, a defoliant that was intended to thin the grass and trees also eliminated Ocracoke's population of frogs. A local legend tells of a Hatteras woman who moved to Ocracoke. After the war, she returned to Hatteras Island with a shoebox to bring a pair of frogs to Ocracoke. She released them in her garden, and they replenished Ocracoke's frog population.

A lasting reminder of the war is the historic British Cemetery. On May 11, 1942, a British vessel was torpedoed and sunk off the North Carolina coast. Several days later, two crew members washed ashore at Ocracoke, followed by two more bodies a week later. Two of the men were identified, and all four were buried on Ocracoke. The Coast Guard still maintains this grave site and holds a memorial service to honor the men each year.

Another historic landmark is the whitewashed Ocracoke lighthouse, built in 1823 and in continuous operation since that time. Lighthouse keepers served until 1946, with Captain Joe Burrus serving from 1929 to 1946. The Burrus family survived three hurricanes at the lighthouse—those of 1933, 1938, and 1944. Local stories tell of islanders floating in boats to the lighthouse and climbing inside for safety during the 1944 storm. Today, the lighthouse is fully automated and is maintained by the Coast Guard.

Hurricanes have always been a part of island life. The worst storms to hit Ocracoke were in 1899 and 1944. Many current residents remember the 1944 storm. The island was completely flooded—homes, docks, and businesses were washed out, and boats and livestock were carried to the tops of small buildings by the rising water. Today's communication system allows for better advance warning, and many people heed the word of the authorities and evacuate the island during dangerous storms. Others say there is no other place they want to live, and if Ocracoke washes away, they want to go with it. In recent years, much damage has been caused by rising water—underground telephone cables and electrical dock wirings have corroded or shorted, many gardens have been destroyed by salt burn, and a great deal of damage has been caused by floating debris. Hurricanes are still a time for those who live on the island to work together to protect the welfare, property, and livelihoods of all.

The Outer Banks have become known as the "Graveyard of the Atlantic" thanks to the fierce winds and storms that travel the coast and the constantly shifting shoals that make navigation difficult. Over forty shipwrecks of boats of more than fifty tons have been recorded off Ocracoke, from early sailing ships to steamers and World War II vessels. Pieces of shipwrecks appear and disappear each year, and diving has recently become a popular activity around Ocracoke.

Another favorite pastime on the island is visiting the Ocracoke ponies, which are believed to be descendants of early shipwrecked horses, probably of Spanish origin. For years the ponies freely roamed the island and village, and in the late 1950s and early 1960s the Ocracoke Boy Scouts were the only mounted troop in the nation. Today, the ponies are maintained by the National Park Service.

The arrival of the National Park Service marked another milestone in the changing of the way of life on Ocracoke. In 1937, Congress authorized the establishment of the National Seashore recreational area, to be permanently preserved as a primitive wilderness area featuring the unique flora and fauna of the Outer Banks. The National Park Service became an active part of life on Ocracoke in 1957 when the state of North Carolina completed the first hard-surfaced road to run the length of the island. Today, the Park Service serves not only the environment but Ocracoke's cultural history as well, with a new Visitor Center designed to acquaint people with the spirit of life on the island.

Fishing and tourism provide livelihoods for the majority of island residents. Many people are self-employed, as Ocracokers tend to be independent by nature. Several new crab and fish houses have provided commercial fishermen with regular outlets in the seafood market. The tourist season continues to expand into the spring and fall, with excellent fishing for bluefish, drum, trout, and flounder in addition to summer catches of cobia, King mackerel, and tuna offshore. Family vacationing is popular in the summer, with swimming, shelling, and sunning on fifteen miles of open beach. The summer season brings many old friends to Ocracoke year after year, but island facilities are sometimes taxed when the population swells to two thousand or more.

Until 1977, Ocracoke's homes and businesses had cisterns to catch rainwater, the island's only source of drinking water. Shallow pumps supplied groundwater for toilets and showers. Today, the island is served by a water system consisting of a deep well and a desalinization plant. This water is pumped to most island residents, and in times of drought or excessive use it has been rationed. It is hoped that the recent expansion of pumping capacity will meet the island's future needs.

Electrical shortages and power fluctuations have been common in recent years. The majority of Ocracoke's electrical power comes to the island through cables that run the hundred-mile length of the Outer Banks and then cross Hatteras Inlet underwater. Ocracoke is frequently without power because of problems many miles away. High winds and salt buildup on the lines also affect electricity on the island. All local homes and cottages have several kerosene lamps and plenty of candles.

Other services on Ocracoke continue to grow in sophistication. Cable television and a town jail have arrived in the last few years. Medical care is provided by a full-time physician's assistant, with emergency service through the Coast Guard. The ferries have turned around to retrieve someone needing medical assistance on numerous occasions, and several babies have been delivered on board. A handful of Ocracoke residents provide the island with its volunteer fire department and rescue squad, and garbage service is provided by local men paid by Hyde County. All garbage is taken to a landfill more than two hours away.

In the wintertime, most activities on Ocracoke are conducted at the schoolhouse or at the Assembly of God or the United Methodist Church, the two houses of worship on the island. Although Ocracoke School is the smallest public school in the state, it offers a wide variety of educational experiences to its students. For the last decade the school has maintained an enrollment of ninety to one hundred students from kindergarten through the twelfth grade. Most grades have six to nine students, and the largest graduating class has been thirteen. Ocracoke School's principal also teaches classes, and all teachers give whatever talents and skills they have to enhance school programs.

Ocracoke is growing and changing, but there is still a strong sense of community on the island. Special events and the unique feeling of the seasons draw people to the island throughout the year—Christmastime, the Crab Festival, fall fishing, the beach in winter. Ocracoke still has no traffic light, no laundromat, no shopping mall, no dentist, no chain store, no funeral home, and no island government. All food, lumber, medical supplies, hardware, and clothes still arrive by ferryboat, weather permitting. Life is very different at sea level. You can relax, meet new people, explore the island, go fishing, sing and dance in the evening, and catch up on the latest fish and weather stories. But best of all, you can put your worries away and feel the power of the wind, sea, and stars.

OCRACOKE PORTRAIT

Spring

Spring is anticipation, a time of preparation with summer just ahead. Spring brings visitors to the island after the winter streets had been quiet and all the cars carried familiar people. The sound of hammers and the smell of paint fill the air, as boats are caulked and given a new coat for another year. Some people go to the pony pen to gather manure for their gardens, while others make last-minute touches on summer businesses and rentals. The phone keeps ringing with long-lost relatives and friends who hope to visit and with inquiries from people searching for places to live and work.

There are small reunions as people return year after year for the Easter sunrise service, the Crab Festival, the Fishing Tournament, and graduation at Ocracoke School. Full moon in May brings fishermen, trout, crabs, and a feeling of romance. Early beach-goers get a start on suntans, and everyone is happy to take off coats and sweaters. There is little talk of the weather, as it is generally mild. Talk is of summer.

"Who do you think will work for that restaurant out there?"

"Have you heard whether they'll be back this year?"

"Anybody catching drum on the point?"

"I'm at peace with myself here. It's a feeling you can't explain."

"The village is the most scenic part of the Outer Banks, and there's no place that comes close to the atmosphere of Ocracoke. There's the sensation of being on an island here. I go to the beach at Ocracoke and it's different. You come over on that ferryboat—I think that does something to your mind. It sets the stage."

"Someone asked me if Ocracoke was like a penal colony. I had to laugh. Utopia it's not, but there is a great sense of community here. I feel like moving to Ocracoke has been my reward. This is where I want to be."

"In the early spring we get those fronts, moving west to east."

"The crabs come in here to spawn, because of the salinity and the ocean currents."

"I don't think Ocracoke is a haven for any one group of people. I think it's a haven for a wide, wide variety of people. I don't think there is one character that typifies Ocracoke. I think for a small town it's probably the most diversified community I've ever been in."

"The new preacher said he reckoned people came to Ocracoke and thought they'd gone to heaven. Well, he said, it might not be heaven, but it's the next thing to it."

"I picked up two hitchhikers in Pennsylvania, eighteen-year-old college students. They said they were out to discover America, and I said, well, you need to see Ocracoke."

Ocracoke Village

"The first families were pilots, in 1717, sent here to pilot ships through the inlet. They would have to lighten the ships—take some of the cargo off—before they could go through the shallow sound. Ocracoke was at the time called 'Pilot Town.' Pilots were Bragg, Gaskill, Gaskins, Garrish, Scarborough, O'Neal, Jackson, Howard, and Williams. They stayed. Other people coming over didn't want to stay. They were frightened to death. They were frightened of the ocean and they were frightened of being so far away from everything."

"There's still a network of people looking out for each other on this island."

Coming in from Pamlico Sound

"It may be only one lane and sand, but Howard Street is probably one of the prettiest streets on the whole East Coast. One of my most vivid memories is coming home from the movies at the Wahab Hotel, now Blackbeard's Lodge. It was always a scary walk up this road. It was so dark and I was all alone. I just walked very fast. My dad used to tell stories about Mag Howard, who used to stand in graveyards. The way I understood the story, she was pretty much kidnapped, I think by some Howard, and brought to Ocracoke as a young girl. I don't know if she was crazy before she got here, but she certainly was later."

"I remember running down Howard Street one night. It was pitch black, no security light then. Running past graveyards and running up on a pony asleep, laying down in the road. I fell over it. I don't know who was scared worse."

Howard Street

The Lighthouse

"There's so much beauty here. Sometimes you don't realize it when you're growing up because it's all you know. The kids have so much freedom here. They can explore on their own."

Albert's Store

Island Pony

"In the late 1950s from age eleven to fourteen I was a mounted Boy Scout. Kids and horses pretty much had unlimited freedom. Horses would ramble around from place to place, just like the dogs and kids. I never felt threatened in my whole life as a kid. I always felt totally and completely safe on this island. We could take the horses and have overnight camp-outs. There were small hunting camps at the hammock opposite where the campground is now. They were abandoned—not being used at that point. The island was all sand. There was no vegetation, all sand flats."

"The weather is such a part of our life. People here know and understand the tremendous *change* that your whole life experiences when the weather changes; it becomes part of you here."

Crossing the Inlet

Riding the Ferry

"Anyone who wishes to feed the sea gulls, please go to the stern of the vessel. This will prevent bird droppings from falling on the vehicles."

"In the spring you're waiting for the tourists to come back. I think the local people begin separating a little bit. They're not as close as in the wintertime. You don't get one day when people appear. They just kind of gradually start coming back until there are a lot of them."

"When people come back in the spring they always are looking for something they've read about in a magazine that we don't carry, probably never will carry. But we're glad just to see them, just to do some business again after a long, quiet winter."

"You need to be in the right place at the right time, using the right method, to catch fish. A lot of it is instincts, too, things that you don't calculate, things that you just have a feeling for—that's a *lot* of it. You're not consciously calculating the outcome, it just seems to come to you. But without all that input, you couldn't have arrived at this intuition."

"Used to be that fishermen only drank a lot when they weren't catching any fish, but now they drink a lot to celebrate when they catch fish, so it's all the time, and it just run us right out of everything. You just can't keep it in stock. They're not quite sympathetic to the fact that we're out of certain liquors, but it's like everything else on Ocracoke. It's difficult to get things here."

"I can hear the sounds of Ocracoke. Ocracoke is memorized."

Surf Rods

Crab Pots

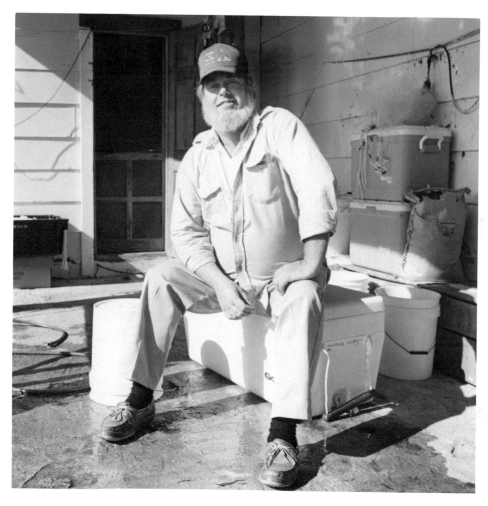

Wayne Teeter, Tradewinds Bait and Tackle

Ikey, Andy, and Monroe

"We've bought us a long-haul net. Mornings that we
don't haul garbage to Manteo, we go fishing."

Deputy Gene Jackson

"When I first went to work we didn't have a building to
work out of. Our office was our vehicles. Then we wound
up with half of that water company building—just big
enough to set the breathalyzer in. When you got in that
place with a coupla drunks rowdy, you had a problem
on your hands. This jail has been long past due."

"Local people aren't impressed by doctors or lawyers or Indian chiefs. It means virtually nothing to them. If they're introduced to somebody who is Dr. John Jones, they call him John. And if he doesn't want to be called John, that's tough. Local people don't express a lot of curiosity about what other people's jobs are. It's who you *are* that matters, not what you *do*."

Teach's Hole Channel

Summertime

Summer is people, recreation, and work. Summer brings tourists, shrimp, clams, fresh figs, garden vegetables, cold beer, beach rides, campfires, greenhead flies, and the midsummer solstice. Activities are plentiful—surfing, swimming, dancing, bike riding, seeing old friends, and making new ones. Sensations are powerful—the hot summer sun burning your shoulders, the warm, friendly breeze, the smell of coconut suntan lotion, the salty taste of the ocean. Sand seems to be everywhere—in your bed, in your bathing suit.

Yet summer gathers momentum and grows *too* hot and *too* humid, careening out of control, not to be stopped until Labor Day. As the season progresses, double shifts come more and more frequently. Finally you have seen enough old friends and made enough new friends and enough money to last through the winter, or so you think. Local fishermen sewing nets in their yards are a sure sign that fall and flounder are truly coming. Now there is talk of weather.

"How 'bout this humidity, seems like the hottest August I can remember."

"Went to the beach, but got run off by greenheads."

"No fish biting yet. Can't wait till fall to catch some drum on the point."

"Probably, if the truth be known, I suspect the summer is the nicest time of the year. Summers are very, very nice on Ocracoke. There's just nothing nicer than getting in your boat and going down to a shoal on a hot, muggy summer day, by yourself or with a few other people, lying down in the water, feeling around for some sand dollars, drinking a cold beer. I don't know that you can beat that."

"I guess I probably enjoy the summer visitors the most because they're such a broad spectrum of people."

"Back from as long as I can remember, dancing on a Saturday night was *the* thing to do on Ocracoke. From the days of the school recreation hall to the early days when the Variety Store had a dance hall, those days were the inspiration for the 3/4 Time Dance Hall today. And it's still obvious on a good Saturday night, with a good band, the enthusiasm of the local crowd is catching. The tourists see that and they end up involved in a fashion you don't often see."

"My father used to say, on Ocracoke you have to be *both* stupid and lazy not to survive. Other than that, everybody makes it on Ocracoke."

"Summertime we get some domestic problems. Couples come down, for some reason they fall out while they're on Ocracoke vacationing. Either the husband throws all of her stuff out of the motel room and takes the car, or she does the same. Crime is coming to Ocracoke. It's to do with the tourists. It's very little in the summertime that you have anything local, some local alcohol and drug offenses, some fighting at the bar."

"You want to meet that one I just met. Wanted to know if we had any work for any of these buildings here. Had two packs of that dry macaroni and a guitar. Damn bums."

"In the summertime on a busy day we'll have about twelve hundred people come in the Visitor Center. On a slow day might be as low as five hundred. And you can bet we talk to about 80 percent of those people one-on-one. Almost everybody in here talks to the Ranger. We've never done a study, but I would estimate we have probably a little more than two questions per person—mostly ecology, natural history, and cultural history questions."

"You know, of course, that Ocracoke is Atlantis."

A Summer Day

The Trolley

"I can't believe this place. Everybody stops and talks to you. It's just like they've known you all their life."

Henry

"What's happened has *happened*, and what's going to happen is *going* to happen, so enjoy the sun on your face right now."

Frances O'Neal

Nathaniel Jackson

Trawler at the Public Docks

Clamming

"It's a long drive for me to Ocracoke, it's 780 miles, and I'll come here for even a three- or four-day weekend. I can be on the island for about ten hours and I'm totally relaxed. The ocean, the surf, the beach, the sun—you can come here and just unwind."

Summertime

Lawton and Connie Howard

"This is where the center of attention always was, down here with the fishing. This dates back to when I was a kid. We came to see the mail boat, the ice, the visitors, and drink the good Cokes. This is where everything happened. Where else can I go and get the fresh breeze, the beauty that's all over Ocracoke? That's what we're noted for—peace, contentment, and fish. Mosquitoes, too—they're part of our heritage."

O'Neal's Dockside

"There's work in all of it, that's for sure. Lots of times you do all this and you don't make nothin'. Then you'll have a good year and then you'll have two, three bad ones. But you work for yourself. That's the whole nut in the shell. You don't have no bosses to answer to. That's the reason I do it. You know, there's a lot of us around here like that."

Dan Garrish Sewing a Net

"When you first move here, you hear somebody talking about something. They speak of it as if it was yesterday and it happened fifty years ago."

"I've heard some stories a hundred times at least, and there are some stories that are repeated every three or four weeks on the docks—what so-and-so said at such and such a time. Some stories seem like they happened yesterday and I know that these people were dead before I was born."

"People have a lot of fun getting reactions out of people when they tell about a scrape that somebody might've gotten in. It's the retelling of it as much as anything that brings a laugh."

Elenora at Her Garage Sale

Summer Cabaret

"Here, if you want, you can be involved with the few
things going on, but otherwise I think it's one of the few
places where there is still individual freedom. More than
that, there's a feeling that people can be themselves."

A Tale of Blackbeard

"I've got an old pickup truck with a gun rack in the back window. I did ride around all summer with a sword in the gun rack. Sometimes two swords."

"People think they're coming to the end of the world, and they're coming to the center of it, they just don't know."

A Summer Path

Fall

Fall is abundance and record-breaking surf fishing. Fall brings gale and hurricane winds, high equinox tides, generous catches of flounder in gill and pound nets, giant mosquitoes, hundreds of ghost crabs, and countless other wonders of nature. The weather is generally clear and beautiful, inspiring old friends to return to the island on annual pilgrimages. Life is a bit more settled than it was in summer, and islanders can again participate in school and community affairs.

Excitement is in the air. People walking or biking through the village carry bags or buckets of fish, and anywhere they go they are likely to bump into a party. The joys and pains of the summer's double shifts are long gone, and everyone talks of closing dates for businesses and restaurants even as they serve lines of waiting fishermen. Winter is close; the first cold snaps bring the best fishing in months. Trucks of firewood arrive almost daily from the mainland. Talk is always of weather.

"Did you hear 'bout the latest tropical storm brewin'?"

"What about that fellow who got trapped on the shoal for two days in that gale?"

"Anybody catching drum on the point?"

"I suspect that most people on Ocracoke would say the fall is the nicest time of the year. It *is* a nice time of year, but that's related to the end of the summer season. You breathe a sigh of relief, and it's the first time you stop and enjoy what's here again. The fall is a relaxing time."

"Ocracoke still has a real strong fishing industry and its own character. It's much more than just a tourist area."

"You either like Ocracoke or you hate it, nothing in between. It's the people and the concern people out here have for others. You can't put it into words. It's very simple, yet it's very beautiful. Here it's hard *not* to enjoy the simple things of life."

"Our friends here range from kids in school up to people in their eighties and have all sorts of interests and every kind of job you can imagine."

"I've never lived any other place that offered what the community is here. This community has become a real support system for me."

"It's just a narrow little island. You go to where Hurricane Gloria blew the dunes out at the north end, and the ocean is *right* there. And you have the sensation that the sound is right on the other side of those bushes—and it is!"

"If you're going to live on the edge, you better be prepared— mentally and physically and with knowledge of your equipment."

Silver Lake

United States Coast Guard Station

Molasses Creek

"We knew that we had to go back to Ohio and sell everything and just come down here and be here. We packed
up the whole truck and came to the Ocracoke campground and lived for eight weeks in the campground and
got jobs. It was perfect. We met tons of good people—
people to sing with, dance with."

Sunrise at Ocracoke Campground

Sunset at South Point

"Yesterday we went fishing. Well, we couldn't keep the lines out on the beach side of South Point—drifting bad with the current and the wind. So we went around to the Point, and we saw this woman a-cranking and we saw it was a *drum*. Boy, I backed in right beside her. We cast out and Maryanna's line kept blowin' acrost everybody's line. Well honey, something *hit*, mine and her at the same time. Boys, we wound it in. It was a drum, a nice fifteen-pound one, but our lines were tangled together *so* bad we've not yet decided which one of us caught it. I swear it's mine and she swears it's hers. But it's good that it happened that way because if one of us had caught one and the other one hadn't, we'd have not come home last night until the other one caught one. We'd a-been there still."

"The inlet will change in a blow."

"Last fall I was working. It was the end of the season, kinda windy day, like today. A couple came in and said, 'Have you seen the fish caught on the beach today?' So I locked the door and I rode out there. I found a hole. Everybody was standing around not catching much. Right at the top of the tide—I like to fish the changing tides. I figured if something's gonna happen, it's gonna happen real soon. I cast out and I had a strike the very first cast. I rebaited and cast out and caught a yearling drum, somewhere between fifteen to twenty pounds. So I packed up my gear and went back to work. . . . No, I didn't grow up fishing, but I hope to someday."

"Fishin' ain't always so hot, so I don't always come back for that—it's the unspoiled beaches."

Phil Styron Checking Nets

Uriah and Sullivan Garrish

"It was in late fall. I was going to Vermont and New Hampshire and New York for my vacation. I had told Babe, Jule's sister, that I was going to New York, and she said, 'I'll go with you.' I said, 'Babe, I'm gonna *fly*,' and she said, 'Well, I'll go with you, I'll try it.'

"I went over to help her pack her stuff and get ready. I said, 'Babe, I'm gonna take a cooler with some seafood.' She said, 'Well, I think I'll take Mamie some seafood.' I said that would be all right.

"The morning we got ready to leave, Brenda and Bill Seymour were going to take us to the airport. Babe said, 'What's in that little box there?' I said, 'Babe, that's my cooler. You forgot your seafood.'

" 'No, I didn't,' she said. 'That man threw it in the trunk.'

"I said, 'Oh my God, no!' When I looked there was that damn frozen flounder—it must have been three feet long! I believe I could have beat a damn nail right in the wall with it, it was so frozen. I said, 'My God, Babe, what are we gonna do with this?'

"She said, 'Well, you told me I could bring it.'

" 'Yea, but I didn't know it was gonna be this big!' And it was whole, wrapped up in brown paper sacks. I said, 'I ain't got no damn choice but to take it with me.'

"Well, we got to the airport. I had her pocketbook and her on one arm and had this bag with a fish tail sticking out of it on the other arm. So we got on the airplane.

"Soon as we got on, I stuck the flounder under the seat. Soon as I did, here comes the stewardess. She said, 'I'm sorry, but you can't have nothing on the floor.'

"I said, 'Lady, if you know what's best for you, you'll leave that right where it is—don't you pull that out of there!'

"She said, 'Well, what is it? You can't have it on the floor.' I said all right and pulled it out. She said, 'You're right. It's better off right where it is.'

"We flew right into La Guardia. I hired a taxi to take Babe and that fish over to Mamie's. It was still frozen when she got there with it. Can you believe that? It was a time."

Jule and His Twenty-one-Pound Flounder

"You can see the fish as they grow through the years. When I first started fishing, there weren't many puppy drum—very rare—and there were a lot of big drum around, which we call 'old' drum. Those fish were hatched in the fifties. They've got a life span, just like you and I, and now they're gone. *Occasionally* you catch an old drum. You can tell him because he looks just like a person—they weather, they age. They'll mature just like people will up to a certain size, then they spend the rest of their life just aging. They may get a little heavier, broader in the shoulders, just fill out. Their fins and noses are worn down. They just look real old."

Clinton Gaskill Cleaning Drum

"I've been here in every hurricane we've had since 1913. The worst was the 1944 hurricane called the 'Great Atlantic'—that was before they started naming them for women. I respect the water. I've lived around it. You know what the water does here: if the wind's to the northwest it comes in from the sound and it washes out to the ocean; and if it's blowin' from the northeast it comes in from the ocean and washes into the sound. It just don't stay. I don't believe that Ocracoke will ever be destroyed by a hurricane. I don't believe that. I think it can be damaged, and if we had one like the 1944 now, it would be a lot worse. In the '44 hurricane there was twelve inches of water in my house. . . . I'm more afraid of a fire than of a hurricane."

Hurricane Weather

Windblown Grave

Flood Tide at the Lighthouse

"People who have just moved here or come to rent a cottage just don't understand life on Ocracoke. You have to be a regular pioneer here. Between the bugs biting, water and power problems, the wind blowin'—and *then* their appliances break! Don't they know we're lucky just to have UPS? They think they come here and everything will get ironed out, but it doesn't. They don't know what real living is—*this is it*. Dreamland is the mainland—this is real life."

Gill Nets Drying

Halloween Night at the Bar

"It's not easy being a sex symbol on Ocracoke."

Thanksgiving

"There is more time here, literally more time. Doing your work, visiting your friends, whatever, can all happen here. Days seem much fuller and much longer. Time on an island. You get to see the sunrise and the sunset, the dawn, and that long, slow period of twilight. The whole passage of time has a much greater sense of flow."

South Point Road

Wintertime

Winter is community. Finally there is time for family and for projects around the home. Winter brings wild ducks and geese and big, salty oysters with lots of hot vinegar to the table. The smell from wood stoves is in the cool, crisp air, and the streets are nearly empty. The island seems resting, quiet. The beach offers solitude, with flocks of migrating geese streaming overhead. Hardy cedars, red-berried yaupon, and golden marsh grass paint the landscape. People entertain themselves with music, shows, plays, and occasional dances, and there is a feeling of connecting with the island's history, for this is how much of the year used to be for islanders. The weather is erratic. People move inside and stay there, and even the fishermen take refuge.

But the solitude can grow lonely, for there is little extra money for diversion and there are few diversions to be found. Picking up the day's mail at 1:30 P.M. provides an occasion for visiting, for sharing local gossip and the latest basketball facts. Plans for summer are discussed and, as always, talk is of weather.

"Did you hear 'bout the latest restaurant business supposed to go up this year?"

"I saw that woman from Florida riding around with you-know-who for the past three days."

"Nor'easter headin' this way, looks bad. Ferries not runnin' today, maybe tomorrow, too."

"In the old days, winter came, you hunkered down, and you survived. Many people didn't have any money, didn't need any money. That's changing. The pressures of modern-day life make you more looking toward the future, and that makes it harder and harder to live in the present."

"Last winter there was the biggest run of scallops that's been here since 1945. Last time before that was 1918."

"I'll tell you, down there around Green Island last winter it was just like somebody had been in there and dumped thirty or forty tractor trailers of scallops. They were that thick. I was down there by myself that first day, there weren't a soul down there. Boy, I was having the best time's ever been. Next day they were like ants down there."

"One question they always ask me as a Ranger, 'Don't you get bored in the wintertime here?' I said, 'Who has time? I have to spend six to eight or nine months dealing with you all, then it takes me three months to catch up, and then you're back again. Isn't that right? That's *right*! My three months I spend doing things I don't get to do, and then 'fore I turn around you're right there a-knocking at the door again, and you just left. No, I don't get bored. I don't have time.' "

"It's a shame that it was ever named Springer's Point, because it should've been Howard's Point instead. This is where the first recorded structure on the island was located, built by William Howard in 1759. Years later this area of Springer's Point is still one of the highest points of land on the island. This is, I'm sure, where the first sand dunes were. I believe that the ocean was much closer at one time."

Springer's Point

Down Point

"Limited hunting is allowed in many national park recreational areas. Hunting was a major industry before the National Park Service was ever involved here. People used to come out here for the great hunting."

"I remember the days, too, that all of the men had to leave the island or starve to death, one or the other. I know one family had four boys and they all couldn't go to school the same day, because they only had two pair of pants. That's a true story."

"I always figured I would retire here, instead of coming back to survive."

"From the first day I got here I felt, 'This is it!' And then I came and spent the winter here. I got around on a bicycle and it was pretty cold that winter, and I hardly knew anybody. So it was a feeling that if I could be happy here then, I could certainly be happy when the weather was nice."

"Wintertime we go back to very simple things. I can buy ten cases of Canadian Mist and ten cases of vodka and maybe two cases of rum and we'd be set for all winter long. We could get by just fine with the local crowd. People don't get upset. They can still remember when we couldn't get liquor here. Even today if there is a fire or emergency, the liquor store closes. It might be closed for twenty minutes, might be five hours."

The Whittlers' Club

"You know, what I enjoy most is the elderly folks on the island. They have a story to tell that nobody else in the world can understand."

Irvin Styron

Family and a Friend

The Community Store

The Church Gets a Tree

"I guess the thing that I remember most as 'Christmas'
is traditions. I like traditions. I like the idea of the Methodist Church having a tree up for 106 years. The tree
this year will be the 107th. I like that."

Santa Arrives on the Ferry

"Christmas is my time of the year. I had about forty-five people to the lighting of the Christmas tree one year at my house. I like the process of getting it ready. It's going toward Victorian style—lots of beads, candles, and shiny ornaments that project a lot of light. I like when you turn the electric lights out and light the candles. A lot of people come back every year to check on it and see it. This is my thing that I enjoy doing, and I'll make time for that. And when I can't, then life's gotten too complicated and I've got to reevaluate life."

Chester and His Tree

PTA Variety Show, Kenny Ballance and Annie Moore Styron

"I was in the seventh grade the year the Rondthalers came to teach. They put on a blackface minstrel, which my mother was in. They had it at the old Wahab Village Theater, now Blackbeard's Lodge. That's my first recollection of any homemade entertainment. From then on we did plays, mostly comedy, and once or twice a year the PTA would have variety shows, and the Civic Club did the womanless weddings. We composed our own words and stole a lot of tunes. If you make believe you know what you're doing, you can fool a lot of people. Of course, it helps when you're a big ham."

"In the winter, the colder it gets, and the later in the winter that it gets, that's when you begin to hear a little more about the gossip things that are going on—talkin' 'bout this one, talkin' 'bout that one."

A Winter Storm

A Winter Freeze

"Ocracoke is in a transition. It's going someplace. Right now it's in a state of changing, and people aren't quite sure how much it's gonna change and they're not quite sure if they're gonna like the change, and of course there are those who are *definitely* not going to like the change. But it's coming. I think it'll take another five or six years to get where it's going."

"Never thought I'd live to see the day on Ocracoke when I'd have to buy sand and water."

"If I was there, I'd fight like hell to keep out the ways of the big city and overdevelopment. It *can* be done—one just has to take a stand."

"Everybody complains about everything being valued so high. They don't want to pay the taxes on it. But when they go to sell it, they want to sell if for four hundred thousand dollars."

"All this runoff on the mainland is choking off all these rivers and there's no place for fish to spawn. Eventually that whole sound might be polluted, and the fish just aren't gonna come in like they did. In the long run there's gonna be an effect."

"A lot of people come down here that don't realize how precious Ocracoke is to some of us. I love the wind, the sea, the old trees."

Sound Shores

"There's no future for all the children here to make a decent good living—unless you're going to be a fisherman, or work with the Park Service, or have a restaurant or something. It sort of goes in generations. You'll have a whole generation that will stay. Then the next generation will split—half will stay and half will go. And the third generation, most of them will leave. It sort of has to be that way to balance things out."

"Ocracoke's gonna change regardless who wants it to or who don't want it to. More people are gonna come every year."

"Nobody owns where the tide ebbs and flows."

"I'm homesick for the island, and I'm here."

"The island is always changing."

"You have to like the environment you're living in in order to live in it happily, and in this case you've got to like water and nature."

"We've got more people here all the time. It's good for the economy, but I don't know if it's good for the spirit."

Seawall

"It's a gamble, this mess. Just like that one year we set those crab pots in February, and it was real warm. We caught good crabs for four days, and the fifth day, went over there to fish 'em and it started breezin' up and blowed so hard we had to quit, all of us. Come back in. That night's the night we had that snowstorm. We went over there two days later and there weren't nothing left. Lost everything we had. It's all a gamble."

United Methodist Church

The North End

"I like the winters. You can walk around the island and not see anybody. You can go out on a winter night a mile and a half away from the ocean and you can hear those waves roaring and look up and see billions of stars in the sky."

"You learn when you fish in a little group that you have a role and you do it without saying. They never did like a lot of talking. Things were generally quiet on the water."

Into the Sound

Quotation Credits

All interviews were collected in the summer and fall of 1987.

Spring

"I'm at peace . . ."	Elenora Hamilton, artist, born on Ocracoke in 1911
"The village is . . ."	P. J. Lewis, Park Ranger
"Someone asked me . . ."	Sandy Berry, new full-time resident of Ocracoke
"In the early spring . . ."	Al Scarborough, business owner, traces his family for six generations on Ocracoke
"The crabs come . . ."	Norman Miller, charter boat Captain, resident since 1973
"I don't think . . ."	P. J. Lewis
"The new preacher . . ."	Islander
"I picked up two . . ."	B. J. Arn-Oelschlegel, business owner, resident for fourteen years
"The first families . . ."	Ellen Marie Fulcher Cloud, business owner, local geneologist, traces her family to early settlers of the island
"There's still a . . ."	Al Scarborough
"It may be only one lane . . ."	Philip Howard, business owner, traces his family to early settlers
"I remember running . . ."	John Ivey Wells, islander, business owner, member of the Ocracoke mounted Boy Scouts in the 1950s
"There's so much . . ."	Hettie Tolson Johnson, islander, business owner
"In the late 1950s . . ."	John Ivey Wells
"The weather is . . ."	Al Scarborough
"Anyone who wishes . . ."	Public announcement on the ferry

"In the spring . . ."	Cliff Heilig, Ocracoke Fire Chief, manager of the liquor store, resident for fourteen years
"When people come back . . ."	Cliff Heilig
"You need to be . . ."	Norman Miller
"Used to be . . ."	Cliff Heilig
"I can hear the sounds . . ."	Sheri Seggerman, longtime visitor, statement in a letter
"We've bought us . . ."	Dan Garrish, islander, fisherman, newest employee of garbage collection service (not in picture)
"When I first . . ."	Gene Jackson, islander, Deputy since 1980
"Local people aren't . . ."	Al Scarborough

Summertime

"Probably, if the truth . . ."	Al Scarborough
"I guess I probably . . ."	Cliff Heilig
"Back from as long . . ."	Jon Wynn, islander, owner of the dance hall
"In the summertime . . ."	P. J. Lewis
"You know, of course, . . ."	Psychic from Tennessee
"Summertime we get . . ."	Gene Jackson
"You want to meet . . ."	Islander, employee at the Community Store
"My father used to say, . . ."	Al Scarborough
"I can't believe . . ."	Tourist, came to the island on a sailboat
"What's happened . . ."	Islander (not pictured)
"It's a long drive . . ."	Paul Stephenson, longtime visitor from Ohio, tent camper

"This is where . . ."   William Arthur O'Neal, spent his childhood summers on Ocracoke, has now retired to the island and works at the family's dockside store

"There's work in all of it, . . ."   Dan Garrish

"When you first move here . . ."   Norman Miller

"I've heard some stories . . ."   Al Scarborough

"People have a lot of fun . . ."   Alton Ballance, islander, schoolteacher, Ocracoke's County Commissioner

"Here, if you want, . . ."   Larry Williams, islander, innkeeper

"I've got an old . . ."   David Senseney, schoolteacher, business owner, resident since 1973 ("Blackbeard" in photograph)

"People think . . ."   Cynthia Mitchell, performing artist, part-time resident

Fall

"I suspect that . . ."   Al Scarborough

"Ocracoke still has . . ."   Howard Bennink, schoolteacher, Park Ranger, resident since 1975

"You either like Ocracoke . . ."   Carlos Umstead, longtime visitor

"Our friends here . . ."   David Senseney

"I've never lived . . ."   Debbie Wells, business owner, resident for ten years

"It's just a narrow . . ."   P. J. Lewis

"If you're going . . ."   Norman Miller

"We knew that we had . . ."   B. J. Arn-Oelschlegel

"Yesterday we went fishing. . . ."   Ellen Marie Fulcher Cloud

"The inlet will change in a blow."   Norman Miller

"Last fall I was working. . . ."   Guy Newell, business owner, resident since 1974

"Fishin' ain't always . . ."   Ed Wanamaker, longtime visitor, tent
camper

"It was in late fall. . . ."   Kenny Ballance, islander, business owner,
Park Ranger

"You can see the fish . . ."   Norman Miller

"I've been here . . ."   Elizabeth Howard, islander, born on
Ocracoke in 1910

"People who have just . . ."   Bill Brelig, owner of the only heating/
air-conditioning/appliance service on
the island

"It's not easy . . ."   Ron Howard, business owner, traces his
family to early island settlers

"There is more time here, . . ."   Cynthia Mitchell

Wintertime

"In the old days, . . ."   Al Scarborough

"Last winter . . ."   Al Scarborough

"I'll tell you, . . ."   Dan Garrish

"One question . . ."   Kenny Ballance

"It's a shame . . ."   Larry Williams

"Limited hunting . . ."   P. J. Lewis

"I remember the days, . . ."   Larry Williams

"I always figured . . ."   Hettie Tolson Johnson

"From the first day . . ."   Barbara Gainey, artist, new full-time
resident

"Wintertime we go . . ."   Cliff Heilig

"You know, what I . . ."   Pat Ware, visitor to Ocracoke for thirty
years

"I guess the thing . . ."   Chester Lynn, islander, business owner

"Christmas is my time . . ."   Chester Lynn

"I was in the seventh grade . . ."	Danny Garrish, islander, entertainer, store manager
"In the winter, . . ."	Larry Williams
"Ocracoke is in a transition. . . ."	Hettie Tolson Johnson
"Never thought I'd live to see . . ."	Longtime island resident
"If I was there, . . ."	Longtime visitor from New Jersey, statement in a letter
"Everybody complains . . ."	Ellen Marie Fulcher Cloud
"All this runoff . . ."	Dan Garrish
"A lot of people . . ."	Pat Ware
"There's no future . . ."	Hettie Tolson Johnson
"Ocracoke's gonna change . . ."	Gene Jackson
"Nobody owns . . ."	Dan Garrish
"I'm homesick for the island, . . ."	Islander
"The island is always changing."	Pat Ware
"You have to like . . ."	Daphne Bennink, spent her childhood summers on Ocracoke, now living full-time on the island
"We've got more people . . ."	Cliff Heilig
"It's a gamble, . . ."	Dan Garrish
"I like the winters. . . ."	Al Scarborough
"You learn when you fish . . ."	Alton Ballance, fished for a year with Uriah and Sullivan Garrish (in picture)